Jane Brocket's CLEVER CONCEPTS

Stickiest, Fluffiest, Crunchiest

Super SUPERLATIVES

Millbrook Press · Minneapolis

KOZATEK

SUPERLATIVES

are words we use to compare things.

2

They help us to describe foods and to say which are the **stickiest**, **crunchiest**, and **fluffiest**.

3

Sticky food glues itself to fingers and faces.
It can be deliciously gloopy and messy to eat.

What's the **stickiest** food you have eaten?

Hold your nose!

Some people say the durian fruit
is the **smelliest** in the world.

But it's not the only food
with a terrible smell!

Crunchy foods are fun to eat because they make so much noise!

Which one do you think is the **crunchiest**?

Some foods have tough skins or hard shells. They protect what's inside and keep it fresh.

The **hardest, toughest** foods can be difficult to cut or open.

Fruit and vegetables can be lumpy, bumpy, spiky, and prickly.

Is the pineapple the **prickliest**?
Or is something else even pricklier?

Light, flaky layers fall off when you bite into the **puffiest, flakiest** pastries.

They flutter and scatter everywhere, like confetti.

15

Gummy candies and doughy crusts take a long time to eat. The **chewiest** ones can make your jaw ache.

16

Do you have a favorite food you like to chew and chew and chew...?

Cooks whisk, whip, bake, and pop ingredients to make them fluffy and airy.

The **fluffiest,
lightest** foods melt
in your mouth.

Wibbly, wobbly foods
make us laugh.

Jell-O and some other desserts wiggle and jiggle when you shake them, but they don't lose their shape.

What is the **wobbliest** food you like to eat?

The **slimiest** foods feel cool and slippery. They are very difficult to hold!

Some have shells that keep them from slithering and sliding out.

Some fruits are super juicy and squirty. We can squeeze them to get fresh, sweet juice.

Which do you think is the **juiciest** of all?

Some pastries and pastas
are spirally and twirly.

But spaghetti may be the **twirliest** of all. It's fun to twizzle and loop it around and around.

The **gooiest** foods are soft and squidgy.

They melt and ooze and spread and stretch.

Do you have a favorite gooey treat?

SUPERLATIVE

foods are super in so many different ways.

The next time you are shopping for groceries or eating a meal, see how many superlative foods you can find.

For
Simon
—J.B.

With many thanks to
Carol Hinz, Danielle Carnito,
and Emily Harris

Text and photographs copyright © 2016 by Jane Brocket

Millbrook Press
A division of Lerner Publishing Group, Inc.
241 First Avenue North
Minneapolis, MN 55401 USA

For reading levels and more information, look up this title at www.lernerbooks.com.

Additional images in this book are used with the permission of: © Torjrtx/Shutterstock.com, p. 6; © Phoebe Brocket, pp. 29 (brownies) and 32 (doughnuts); © iStockphoto.com/eliane (cardboard background); © iStockphoto.com/Winston Davidian (textured paper background).

Main body text set in Chaloops Regular 24/32.
Typeface provided by Chank.

Library of Congress Cataloging-in-Publication Data

Cataloging-in-Publication Data for *Stickiest, Fluffiest, Crunchiest: Super Superlatives* is on file at the Library of Congress.
ISBN: 978-1-4677-9241-7 (LB)
ISBN: 978-1-4677-9268-4 (EB)

Manufactured in the United States of America
1 – PC – 7/15/15